Life In Poetry Two

Eliza Rojas

Presentation by *BookLeaf Publishing*

Web: www.bookleafpub.com

E-mail: info@bookleafpub.com

ISBN: 9789363314597

First edition 2024

*I want to dedicate this book to my children
whom I love very much. They inspire to
keep writing poetry regardless of whatever
I am going through in life. They are my
motivation to everything I do in life.*

ACKNOWLEDGEMENT

I would like to acknowledge Book Leaf Publishing because without their help I would not be able to publish this book.

PREFACE

This book is the second book of my two book series "Life In Poetry". This book is written to describe significant events that have taken place in my personal life. Some of these poems are just written in general. This book was written to help relate to other readers, of all ages.

To My Daughter

Babygirl I love you so so much,
Having you
I was full of luck,
You are my sweet angel,
I know I am away from you,
It hurts me alot,
Because I want to be there with you,
I see you growing into a beautiful young lady!
You are so smart,
Everything you know, everything you say,
I love you so much,
I can't wait to see what you will one day
become,
I think you will be an art teacher, since you
really love art,
Whatever you decide to be, I will be there,
Always by your side,
In spirits and in person, I will always be your
guide,
I cannot wait to move back to Florida so that I
can be with you,
The fun we will have,
The shopping we will do,
I love you little girl,
I am so so proud of you!

To My Son

Son, the moment you were born,
I knew my life had once again changed,
There was a new reason to continue moving
forward with life,
You had the most beautiful skin,
Melanin,
You loved to smile,
Even though yet you didn't have teeth,
It was the most precious thing,
You were a beautiful human being,
One thing I remember,
You were in my belly,
And you suddenly began to run,
I could feel so many steps,
In my belly you were having fun,
My second love,
My son,
I guess it's true when they say,
God gives you a son for a reason,
To find the meaning of true love,
In every season,
Son you had once again changed my life,
If I could give you life advice, it is to
always be yourself,
In all circumstances,

know your true self,
And I will always be there,
I love you my brown chocolate baby,
You have no idea how happy you make me!

Little Girl

Little girl scared to stay alone,
her stepdad abuses her,
and her mother doesn't know,
She scries when her mom leaves to work,
how can her mom not possibly know?
She hides away from him,
Behind wood cabinets,
He immediately looks around for her,
Then he takes her to the room,
And abuses her,
Little girl doesn't know what to do,
he threatens her and she is scared,
He has instilled fear in her,
And she knows she cannot tell her mom,
He threatens to and punches her,
And the little girl cries for help,
But, there is no one there,
Little girl all alone,
Trapped in her scary world.

Homeless

I remember my mom didn't know what to do,
step dad was on the run,
running from the cops,
It all happened so quick,
One day after the next,
We were homeless,
A mother of four kids,
I remember mom baked a pie with only a few
ingredients,
It's all the food we had,
She baked it with pecans,
And everything else she could find,
At this point it didn't matter,
as long,
as we could eat, we didn't mind,
But where could we go?
The bills were piling up,
My brothers and I had to go to school,
We didn't have a car,
It was so sad,
What would my mom do, to take care of all of
us?
My mother is all we had.

Lost Love

I am constantly looking for the love I have lost,
I don't know why,
But I know that I must,
It's all that I have,
Now that you're gone,
I think of you often,
I still love you to death,
I wish things were different,
But instead,
Everything seems confusing,
I know this is what it feels like to have lost love,
But I hope you know you will always be in my
heart.
My lost love.

To my Dad

I never got to know you,
I know that I got to meet you,
I know that I was nine months old when you
went away,
Something happened,
And you got locked away,
For the two times I saw you, I don't remember
your face,
I didn't know what you looked like, till the other
day,
One of my uncles sent me a picture of you,
I see that you have aged,
Mom doesn't show me pictures of you,
I've only seen one or two,
I remember mom would treat me so bad
sometimes,
She would tell me all sorts of things,
And then I always wished you were there,
I always needed a good father figure,
but you were never there,
I spent a long time crying for you,
Nobody cared,
You didn't get to see me grown
And it hurts,
And now you want to come into our lives,

However, you still don't seem to care,
I don't know how to feel,
Should I ignore you or should I talk to you?
I think I know the answer,
I just hope you are there for the right reasons,
And it's not just money that you are needing.

I'm Sorry Mama

Mama I love you,
I know that I am hard to handle,
I am sorry that I am not the daughter
you want me to be,
In my eyes,
there is no perfection,
You always tell me that I am rebellious,
But mama my character, and my feelings,
Make me who I am,
I want you to know that I am sorry,
for everything I have said to you,
I know I can't take back all those words,
Even when I was a teenager,
Remember I told you I hated you,
But you used to treat me so bad,
It was so hard for me to understand you,
I want to tell you that I love you,
You're all that I have left in this world,
Dad isn't there,
He never cared,
So I always pray for you,
I wish I had a majic wand to heal you,
Sadly life doesn't work that way,
But just know God's always got you,
he knows what you're going through,

He's with you every step,
know this,
Mama I will always love you.

Love

What is love?
I never really knew the meaning of love,
I thought I did,
But I had to watch exactly what was going on,
realizing,
He didn't love me as much as I loved him,
I am a passionate person,
and maybe that's why I cared more than him,
I don't want to ever love like that again,
The next time love comes around,
I will make sure,
that person loves me more,
I cannot love him more,
But I can sure love in return,
Love is beautiful if you let love be,
It will open doors, for everything,
that you cannot see,
Sometimes though love is blind,
And we cannot see,
When love isn't meant to be,
But love is beautiful if you let it,
In every way,
Because where there is a will, there is a way.
This is love I guess.

To my Abusive Step Dad

There is not a lot of words I want to say,
because I am disgusted,
of the person you were,
You abused me as a child,
I still remember,
I can never forget those days, they are in my
mind,
Stenciled,
In a picture,
But I now understand that I had to go through
that,
Everything I went through,
Is a part of my path,
It made me who I am,
And everything you did to my mom,
you got what you deserved,
When you got locked up,
Even though they let you out early,
It was kinda messed up,
I would have left you in there for life,
But I guess life must go on,
You got what you deserved,
Karma is a bitch,
I heard you are crazy,
And lost in the streets,
Well everything happens for reasons,
one cannot see

Chosen

I didn't know that I was chosen until I noticed
that I always suffered,
Ever since I was a little girl,
But back then I didn't know the answer,
Why I was chosen to be one of "the chosen
ones"
I still can't fathom,
My life has been very difficult,
It's never been easy,
It seems like there is always an issue
Why I am always uneasy,
I don't know what my path in life is,
but I know that one day I will know,
I believe in God deeply,
I know that he's always with me,
Being chosen is very hard,
While everyone else has an easier journey,
We have a harder path,
But there is a reason for everything,
God does what he does,
He knows,
The worst,
And the best,
He gives us a lot of tests,
I guess that's why we are chosen.

I'm Sorry

I'm sorry that I couldn't be the person you
wanted me to be,
I tried so hard,
But it wasn't easy,
I listened to what you wanted of me,
And I tried to do all those things,
It was all to crazy,
I am sorry that you had to follow me,
When I was in the military,
I just wanted a better life,
than what I grew up with,
I had to make a sacrifice,
But I also wanted us to be together,
I just couldn't yet quit what I started,
We also needed money,
And I had no plans of anything,
I am sorry for everything bad that happened,
The mistakes I made,
Everything I ever did,
The things that I said,
I'm sorry that things happened
the way they did,
We can never forget.

In my Head

Sometimes I get stuck in my head,
My thoughts are not straight,
It is what I do not get,
I will let my emotions get ahold of me,
Without medication, I am nothing,
I cannot survive without meds,
My brain has a chemical imbalance,
Which I have tried to fix,
But I cannot do it,
When I am in my head,
I forget everything,
dissociation hits,
And the thoughts stay lingering,
I try to think differently,
But it's not that easy,
I hate being in my head.

Addiction

Watching you everyday drinking,
3-4 bottles of wine a day,
or a bottle of vodka,
You had me thinking,
When you drinked, you acted different,
You started being aggressive,
Then aggressive turned into abusive,
It was a pattern
And I became used to it,
I always wanted to help you,
But I didn't know how,
I tried everything,
And somehow, nothing worked,
Then everything got worse,
Addiction is a very serious thing,
You do not realize at the moment what is,
happening,
You hurt people you love,
Even if you don't want to,
The mind isn't there,
It's not fair,
I wish I could have done something to take your
pain away,
But you didn't let me,
You just pushed me away.

I still Do

I want you to know that I still love you,
And I know you don't care,
Because when I text,
You don't answer,
And when I call you, you tell me,
"Call later",
I would do anything for you to care,
But I cannot force something that is no longer
there,
I have learned, if you have to force it,
it's not real,
3 years ago we seperated, but I love you as it
was the first day I met you,
Something about you,
Is so special,
You are my other half,
You have what I lack,
But I think you have moved on,
You totally ignore me,
I don't think you have the same love for me,
People always say that men move on faster than
women,
But my love for you lingers,
And it always will,
I told myself I cannot be selfish with you,

I must release you so that you can do what you
want to do,
That's how much I still love you,
If you think I don't, I still do.

Domestic Violence

I remember the words you used to call me,
Out of anger you would verbally assault me,
You would make comments about my weight,
And that would hurt me,
You would say that I was fat,
And you wanted me to be skinny,
But I just couldn't understand that,
Then you would go for the liquor,
Buying multiple bottles at a time,
you would get so aggressive,
And I couldn't do anything about it,
The moment I tried to help you,
You would get so pissed,
So I had to stop it,
The abuse was so immense,
It was indeed domestic violence,
I never thought I would go through this,
Never in my mind,
Thought I would go through this in life,
For any women that are experiencing this,
get out.
Because it gets worse,
One small argument, will turn so big,
One small act of physical abuse,
Turns way worse,
Get out before it's too late.

When a chosen one makes a Mistake

When a chosen one makes a mistake,
all hell brakes loose,
It's all a call for trouble,
People don't know,
But chosen ones have it worse,
If we make a mistake everything,
starts crumbling down,
Little by little,
Sound by sound,
It's almost as if it's a curse,
The spiritual attacks start coming,
In every bad dream,
It feels like someone is after you,
And everything you do,
Being a chosen one is not easy at all,
We literally have to remain super strong.

One Day

I hope one day I get to be loved the right way,
may the right one come by,
And stay,
One that also loves my kids,
I hope one day I get to relax and just be a mom.
Not be so chaotic,
That everything seems to go wrong,
I hope one day I know what true love feels like,
Maybe I have already experienced it,
But it past by me,
True love is hard to find,
But with the right person it should be fine,
You won't have to try so hard,
They will get you,
From the start,
You will feel safe in every which way,
One day.

Beautiful Butterfly

Beautiful butterfly with your colorful wings,
You fly everywhere and seek sweet things,
You start as a cocoon,
And later develop into something new,
Beautiful butterfly you give the world color,
Flying everywhere,
So wonderful.

What is heaven like?

I wonder what heaven is like?
Is there angels flying all over the sky?
Are there two different sides?
Where the angels and the demons lie?
Is it a beautiful place, where it's full of peace?
And nothing goes wrong?
I wonder if heaven is for everyone?
Or only a select few,
I wonder if heaven is truly beautiful?

Spiritual Warfare

Have you ever been attacked by spirits in your
dreams?
You would have scary nightmares
and see scary things,
There's a spiritual warfare going on,
 The devil will try to attack you,
When he can't get to you,
 he uses the people around you,
The people you love the most,
Doesn't matter at what cost,
You must not pay attention to these attacks,
Because God has your back,
Let him fight those battles,
It is not your battle,
spiritual warfare.

Healing childhood Trauma

For many people their child hood was not good,
They experienced alot,
Lots that no one can really understand,
From the start of when they were young,
These people had it hard,
And now it is time to grow up,
And they must try to heal that childhood trauma,
This is so hard,
Because often times than not,
People don't know how to start,
The healing process needs to begin,
With every decision,
And all that the heart brings,
I am still healing my childhood trauma,
It has been so long,
But I know that the show must go on,
I have two kids that look up to me,
I have no choice than to be strong for them
Healing childhood trauma starts within me.